Animals of Ohio Coloring Book with Poems, Facts, and Mazes

2019

Animals of Ohio Coloring Book with Poems, Facts, and Mazes was created for the Stark County Park District, 2019.

Poetry © by David B. McCoy

Images and mazes allowed as this is a noncommercial publication. Main sites:
dltk-kids.com
crayola.com
animaljr.com
woojr.com
clipart-library.com
olphreunion.org

Dedicated to Brian, Ayla, and Aiden.

ANTS like to hang out with friends
and live in homes known as nests.
But sometimes, they want their beds
to be in *our* home as an unwelcomed guest.

FACT
A single ant can carry 50 times its own bodyweight.

Help the animals find their food!

BEARS in the city are so rare,
not that you can find them anywhere,
that's because they hate how car horns blare—
preferring to live in quiet solitaire.

FACT
Teddy bears were named after U.S. President
Theodore "Teddy" Roosevelt.

Help the animals find their food!

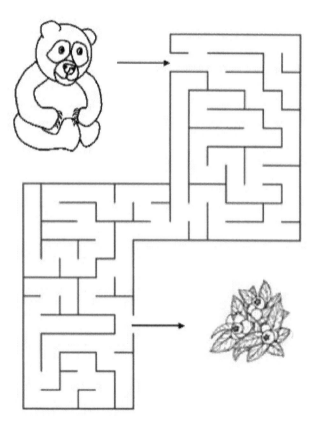

Living in any freshwater stream
is the little crusty CRAYFISH.
But catching one is harder than it seems—
it'll disappear with a backward *swish*.

FACT
All of the "legs" of the crayfish can grow back if they are broken off.

Help the animals find their food!

Once while out walking in the spring of the year,
when the weather was rather warm and clear,
I crossed paths with a herd of DEER,
who must have wondered how I got so near.

FACT
Deer are the only group of animals in the world to have antlers that grow back and fall off each year.

EELS to some are of great appeal
and end up being their dinner meal.
But when I meet one—I turn on my heels
and let out a loud squeal.

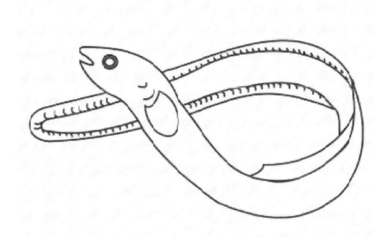

FACT
Even though the eel looks like a snake it is really a fish.

Help the animals find their food!

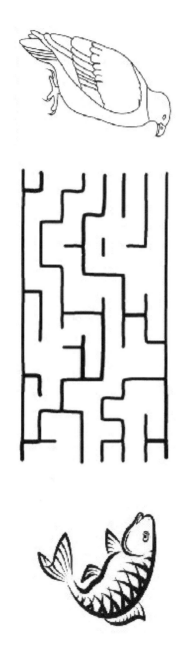

The family of FROGS
who lives in the bog,
and bark like wild dogs,
think of it more as dialogue.

FACT
Some frog calls can be heard up to a mile away.

Help the animals find their food!

I can't think of what a GOAT
could possibly find to gloat
about, except perhaps those awful notes
he admits from his straining throat.

FACT
Goats can be taught their name and to come when
called.

Help the animals find their food!

Darting that way ... Darting this way.
Hovering stock-still ... HUMMINGBIRDS,
at 30 miles per hour, may fly away—
or even backwards when undeterred.

FACT
Hummingbirds cannot walk or hop, though their feet
can be used to scoot sideways while they are perched.

An INSECT is a tiny bug
you wouldn't want to hug,
but you just might like to collect
and keep in a big ole jug.

FACT
There are 1900 types of edible insects on Earth.

At winter's first snow, look for
the dark-eyed JUNCO to appear
in search of fallen seeds-galore
before returning north for the coming year.

FACT
The dark-eyed junco's nickname, "Snowbird," is for
its winter-weather coloration and because it appears
at feeders at the first snowfall.

Help the animals find their food!

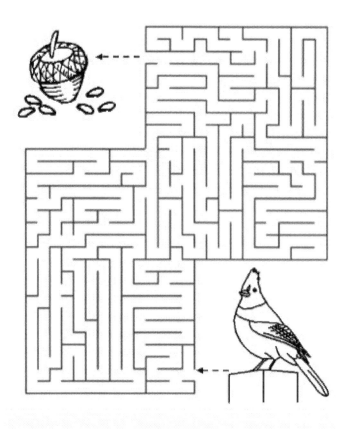

The little falcon with two
stripes on its face and a *klee!...klee...klee* call
is the American KESTREL, who
so quickly from out the sky can fall.

FACT
The American kestrel hunts mostly by watching from a
high perch, then swooping down to capture prey.

LADYBUG! Ladybug!
Bring us some luck.
Ladybug! Ladybug!
Leave us starstruck.

FACT
Some cultures believe ladybugs are a sign of good luck.

Swimming so close to the shoreline—
by the hundreds—if not many more—
are tiny MINNOWS. And being streamlined,
they swim as if they're on a dance floor.

FACT
Minnows have teeth in their throats instead of the
mouths.

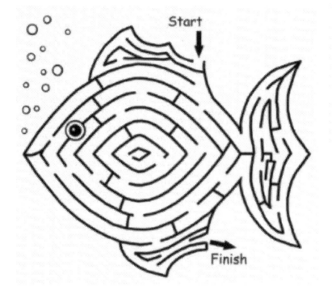

NIGHTCRAWLERS stay underground
until the sun sets and the grass
is wet from dew—but around
nighttime, they emerge in a great mass.

FACT
Nightcrawlers in your lawn is an indication that
your lawn is healthy.

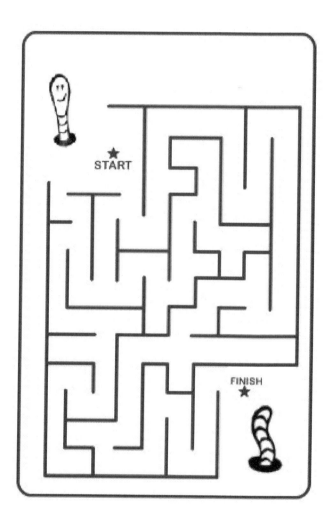

There's an OPOSSUM asleep on the floor.
He won't wake when I give him a nudge
or even when I open the door.
Perhaps I should offer him a piece of fudge.

FACT
Opossums, when threatened, "play possum" and act as if they are dead.

Help the animals find their food!

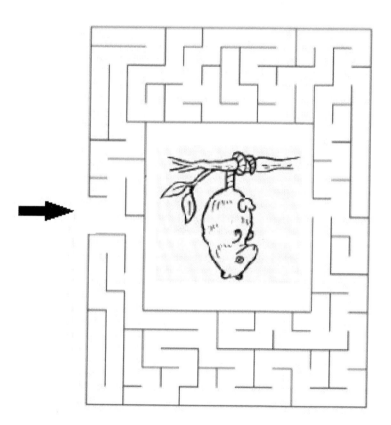

There's a PIG walking down the street—
he doesn't seem to be in any hurry
but he clearly doesn't like the heat
and wishes he were back on the farm.

FACT
A pig's squeal is louder than a jet engine.

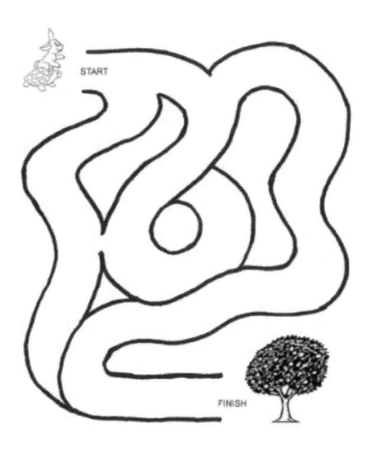

The bird with tiny wings and tail
is known as the bobwhite QUAIL
and repeats, with great delight,
his funny name—Bob-White! Bob-White!

FACT
The males try to attract the females by their
characteristic "bob-white" calls during early springtime.

Help the animals find their food!

Curled up asleep all afternoon
is the masked—face RACCOON.
But at night under a bright moon,
he likes to go fishing at the lagoon.

FACT

Black markings that fall across their eyes, works just
like the black stickers athletes wear under their eyes:
The dark color absorbs incoming light, reducing
glare that would otherwise bounce into their eyes
and obstruct their vision.

Help the animals find their food!

Small enough to fit in your shoe
(it needn't matter if old or new,
or even if in far-off Peru)
is the velvety, short-tailed SHREW.

FACT
Shrews are easily startled and will jump, faint, or drop
dead at a sudden noise.

Help the animals find their food!

This is my ode
to the poor old TOAD
who tried to be so bold
and hopped out onto the road.

FACT
Toad's skin lets out a bitter taste and smell that
burns the eyes and noses of its predators, much like
a skunk does.

Help the animals find their food!

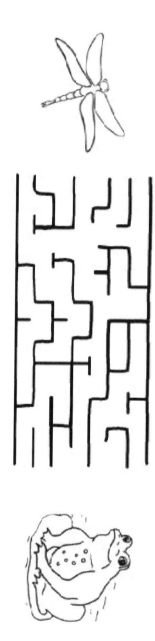

While you might think to look on sand
for the UPLAND SANDPIPER—they instead prefer
an upland meadow to make their stand
before heading south eight months of the year.

FACT
When disturbed, upland sandpipers will run a short
distance and "freeze" in an attempt to blend into
surrounding habitat and confuse a predator.

The bald, reddish-head of the VULTURE
may look awfully peculiar,
but when it soars in circular
formations, it looks almost spectacular.

FACT
Vultures are also known as buzzards. Every March
15, like clockwork, buzzards return to Hinckley,
Ohio after their winter vacations.

WALLEYE to some may sound like
and eye on a wall, but it's a fish
many, for a great distance, will hike
in order to catch because they're *D-Lish*.

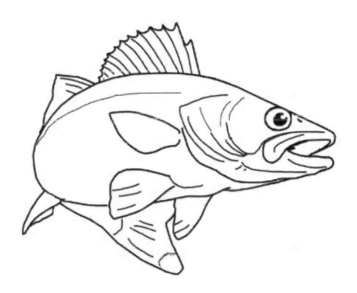

FACT
Walleye is the state fish of Ohio.

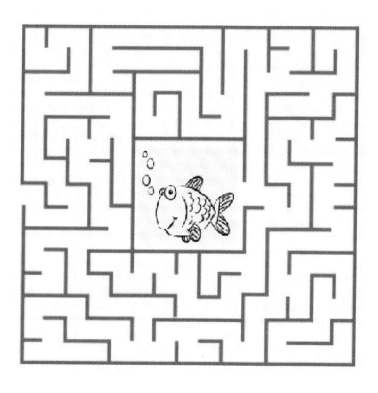

It does indeed seem unusual
that there exists not one animal,
even among those with specks,
with the name which starts with X.

FACT
Actually, there are at least four animals that start
with X, but none live in Ohio.

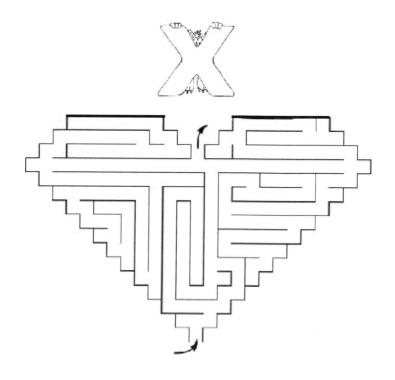

The YELLOWTHROAT is a bird who flitters
about with its brightly colored feathers
in wetlands and cattail marches
where artists go to draw lively sketches.

FACT
The male's distinctive *wich-i-ty wich-i-ty wich-i-ty*
song makes it an easily identified warbler.

ZEBRA mussels are new in town—
hitched rides on boats from afar.
Now they caused many folks to frown
because they're as hard to remove as tar.

FACT
The zebra mussel was originally native to the lakes
of southern Russia and Ukraine.

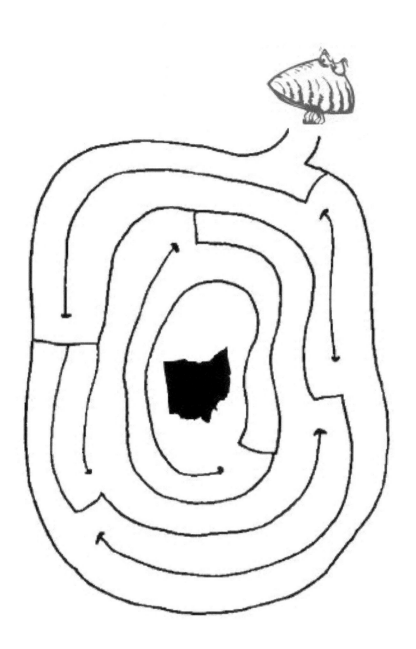

David McCoy and his wife, Jill, live on the property that adjoins Sippo Lake Park.

Made in the USA
Lexington, KY
23 August 2019